Keys to Teaching
Junior High School Music

PRINTED IN U.S.A.

P-5382

Keys to Teaching
Junior High School Music

by

HARRIET NORDHOLM

Department of Music Education

University of Miami

Coral Gables, Florida

and

RUTH V. BAKEWELL

Assistant Supervisor of Music

Billings Public Schools

Billings, Montana

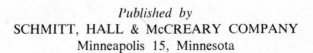

Published by

SCHMITT, HALL & McCREARY COMPANY

Minneapolis 15, Minnesota

ACKNOWLEDGMENTS

Grateful acknowledgment is expressed to the following people: Mr. Charles R. Cutts; Supervisor of Music, Billings, Montana; Miss Lena B. Grinley, Austin Public Schools, Austin, Minnesota; Mrs. Alice Doll Nelson, Walter French Junior High School, Lansing, Michigan; Mr. Lloyd Oakland, Montana State University, Missoula, Montana; and Miss Martha White, Michigan State College, East Lansing, Michigan.

CONTENTS

ACKNOWLEDGMENTS

Grateful acknowledgment is expressed to the following people: Mr. Charles R. Cutts, Supervisor of Music, Billings, Montana; Miss Lena B. Grinley, Austin Public Schools, Austin, Minnesota; Mrs. Alice Doll Nelson, Walter French Junior High School, Lansing, Michigan; Mr. Lloyd Oakland, Montana State University, Missoula, Montana; and Miss Martha White, Michigan State College, East Lansing, Michigan.

Foreword

Miss Harriet Nordholm, who is a staff member at Michigan State College, is widely known for her inspiring work with children and teachers. For many years she has been a successful music supervisor; she has deep understanding concerning teacher education problems; she is much in demand throughout the country as a lecturer-demonstrator. She is co-author with Carl O. Thompson of the book *Keys To Teaching Elementary School Music;* she has been a guest instructor at summer sessions of Northwestern University, the University of Minnesota, and other teacher-training institutions.

It was this writer's privilege, while teaching in summer school at Montana State University, to have her attention directed toward a thesis presented by Miss Ruth Bakewell, a teacher in the public schools of Billings, Montana. The work represented long and careful research which resulted in a great collection of source materials organized into units for music teaching in the junior high school. It was mainly geared to the general music class where the demand for such material is very great. Miss Bakewell was urged to try to market what she had accomplished. The result has been the co-authorship with Miss Nordholm in this volume.

The contribution of each has been significant—Miss Nordholm's because of her insight into problems of junior high school music teaching, Miss Bakewell's because of her imaginative and careful research in planning source units. The work is both practical and inspirational and is so presented that it will be a valuable guide to young musicians preparing for the field of teaching and to in-service teachers as well. It defines the problems of both the required and the elective programs in a straight-forward manner. It maintains a creative and an appreciative approach in the solution of the problems. It stimulates interest in the relationship of music to the rest of the curriculum. It points the way to happy, profitable, stimulating classroom experiences within the interest and capacities of young people in any situation!

Delinda Roggensack
Associate Professor of Music Education
Cornell College
Mount Vernon, Iowa

Introduction

In guiding the musical growth of adolescent boys and girls, the teacher should strive for a development within each student in the physical, social, emotional, spiritual, and aesthetic areas. These young people possess a wide variety of abilities and interests; they have very positive likes and dislikes even though there is sometimes lack of uniformity in their musical preparation. Because of this, the teacher must provide a program rich in activities so there always may be a genuine enjoyment of music by the students.

These young people should be led to realize that music is a language—a natural, universal expression of feeling of all mankind from the primitive to the most civilized. Music is not to be considered as something set apart from them, but as something which has personal meaning and use in their everyday life. The students meet people of the world and learn to appreciate them through music because it portrays their customs, cultures, dress, climate, industries, resources, religions, political beliefs, and ideals.

Generally speaking, there is great interest in elementary school music and in high school performing groups. Unfortunately, it is sometimes true that there is a disinterest on the part of teen-agers in junior high school music. On occasion, remarks are made which would indicate that junior high school students are at a difficult age. Where does the fault lie? Certainly not with the boys and girls. It may be that the teacher has difficulty understanding these sometimes unpredictable but very interesting teen-agers. It may be that suitable materials have not been selected.

How then, can the situation be improved? It must be remembered at all times that we are not teaching music, but we are teaching boys and girls. We do not measure our success in terms of perfection, but rather in terms of child growth and development. We must permit the student to use his own initiative; we must encourage him to participate in the planning of activities.

The difficult student will participate in music when he feels like it; when things are presented which are of interest to him. The teacher must have dozens of plans at his disposal; he must be a story-teller and a humorist; he must be firm but pleasant; he must have a sincere affection for young people and a deep understanding of how they respond to music; he must know materials and how to use them.

There are three ways to use music: to perform it; to listen to it; to create it. The teacher must give opportunity for each student to do all of these things.

There should be an apparent development of correlation between life in school and life out of school including such activities as concerts, radio, television, movies, plays, travel, and reading. Attention should be called to music as it is used in the motion picture industry and in television. The carry-over of his musical growth into everyday life should be the outcome of each student's in-school musical experiences.

General Music Classes in the Seventh and Eighth Grades

General Music Classes in the Seventh and Eighth Grades

The general music class consists of a heterogeneous group of boys and girls pursuing the various phases of music education during a required period of time. Because of the diverse interests of the class, work must be planned so as to permit each student to accomplish something tangible all of the time. A busy student has little opportunity to get into mischief.

The teacher of the general music classes, in planning his work, should correlate music activities with academic procedures. In schools where there is a core curriculum this is a "must." Other staff members should be consulted so that material can be adjusted to fit the general theme of the core.

Since the unit or topic approach is an effective aid in teaching music on the junior high school level, ten units have been included in the text. It is not necessary to cover all of them. Choices can be made and portions of the units can be extended and amplified to meet the needs and interests of specific groups. Units designated for seventh grade can be adapted to eighth grade and vice versa, depending upon local situations.

Other unit possibilities which could be worked out are: Our Home Town or Community, Ways of Life of Our Australian and New Zealand Neighbors, and One World Through Books. Still others might be developed from songs, recordings, books, and other in-school and out-of-school activities and experiences. Whatever units are used, there must be much significant planning and research by both teacher and students to make each lesson in the general music class interesting, worthwhile, and meaningful.

Occasionally, as an outgrowth of the regular classroom work, a program on one of the units might be given at an assembly.

While singing will perhaps always remain the core of the music education program, the general music class should emphasize something more than singing. Consequently each unit also includes ample opportunities for listening, rhythmic, and creative experiences.

Whenever possible, students should be encouraged to bring in material which can be used in the unit studies. Educational pursuits in junior high school come alive when boys and girls work with their music teacher, the music teacher works with teachers in other subject areas, and those teachers in turn work with their pupils. The inevitable outcome will be richer experiences and greater enjoyment of life.

SUGGESTIONS AND PROCEDURES

Singing

In choral music the first concern is to achieve beautiful singing. Young people have a natural impulse and desire to sing. It is the teacher's obligation to do all that he can to develop that impulse and desire so that the student, through the singing of a song, can have an educational experience. Constant emphasis should be given to good posture, correct breathing, enunciation, and artistic interpretation.

There should be a great deal of rote* singing in seventh and eighth grades. The following procedure may be used for teaching by rote:

1. Discuss the song briefly.
2. Sing the song to the group artistically, using good tone, careful diction, logical phrasing, and good interpretation. Or play the song on the piano or play a recording of it.
3. Question the class briefly regarding their understanding and enjoyment of the song.
4. Lead the students to join gradually and naturally in singing. Withdraw little by little until they can sing the song independently.

* Singing by imitation.

5. Have them sing the entire song, giving them assistance only when they need it. Artistic interpretation should be emphasized. The same plan could be followed in teaching a two or three-part song except that the parts may need to be taught separately. It is suggested that a student change from alto to soprano and vice versa only when new songs are read.

If teen-agers have had an adequate elementary music background, they will be able to read music easily and well. The following procedure may be used in presenting a song by the reading method.

1. Scan the words of the song in correct meter. If a difficult rhythm figure is encountered, or if, occasionally, the students need and want to do something a bit different with a song, part or all of the group may step off the rhythm of the song using the modified Dalcroze movements given at the bottom of this page.
2. Try reading the song at sight using words. Motives or phrases that prove difficult may be sung by syllables, numbers, or letters. Sing them with "loo", then once again with the words.
3. Watch the dynamic markings and interpret the song artistically.

Dalcroze Movements

The modified Dalcroze *foot* movements are as follows:

Whole note: *step* with left foot, bring right foot *front,* bring right foot out to the *side,* bring right foot *back* to meet left foot, and vice versa.

Dotted half note: *step* with left foot, bring right foot out to the *side,* bring right foot *back* to left foot, and vice versa.

Half note: *step* with left foot, *bend* right knee, and vice versa.

Quarter note: walk.

Eighth note: run.

Sixteenth, thirty-second notes, and triplets: fast run.

The simplified Dalcroze *arm* movements follow the basic beat of the music as follows:

$\dfrac{4}{4}$
$\begin{cases} \text{count 1: both arms plunged down} \\ \text{count 2: both arms over chest} \\ \text{count 3: both arms brought out to either side} \\ \text{count 4: both arms in place at sides} \end{cases}$

$\dfrac{3}{4}$
$\begin{cases} \text{count 1: both arms plunged down} \\ \text{count 2: both arms brought out to either side} \\ \text{count 3: both arms in place} \end{cases}$

$\dfrac{2}{4}$
$\begin{cases} \text{count 1: both arms plunged down} \\ \text{count 2: both arms back up in place} \end{cases}$

A rhythmically alert class will be able to combine the foot and arm movements. If they have difficulty putting the two together, have the students do the foot movements while singing the song, do the arm movements while singing the song, then put the foot and arm movements together.

SIGHT-SINGING.   If a class at the junior high school level cannot sight-read music either by syllables, numbers or letters, it is questionable whether the group should be taught reading skills. Students who, either through lack of opportunity or lack of ability, have come up through the elementary grades without mastering the music reading skill may, if made to do so now, develop an apathy or even a hearty dislike for music. If the class cannot sight-read, the wise teacher will encourage singing by rote or singing by position. He may point out the rise and fall of melody, indicating this through moving his hand in the direction in which the melody moves; he may conduct; he may lightly clap his hands. In other words, he will do all that he can to foster musical growth while keeping alive within each student a sincere enthusiasm for singing.

TWO AND THREE-PART SINGING. When reading two and three-part music, it is very important to keep all parts moving simultaneously. If individual parts need a great deal of assistance, very likely the group is not ready to sing in parts or the song chosen is too difficult.

Occasionally chord progressions in the song may be taken out and studied separately. This will ease the difficulty and give a feeling of security when the song is read again. Humming the tones and singing with "loo" or vowels (ah, oh, oo, etc.) will lead naturally into good tone production. Keep isolated drills, exercises, and vocalization to a minimum. Assume that a group can do an assigned job. When additional assistance needs to be given, use the song itself rather than formalized drills.

THE MINOR MODE. Have the students sing several songs in the minor mode by rote. Play several recordings in the minor mode. This will establish the mood for minor songs.

To introduce the *normal minor* scale use the following or any other simple one-part minor song:

1. Write the E♭ major scale on the blackboard. Have the class sing this scale with syllables.

2. Erase *ti* and *do* at the top of the scale, then add notes for *la* and *ti* at the beginning of the scale. The normal minor scale will appear like this:

KEY OF C MINOR (NORMAL MINOR)

LA	TI	DO	RE	MI	FA	SO	LA
6	7	1	2	3	4	5	6
C	D	Eb	F	G	Ab	Bb	C

3. Have the class sing the normal minor scale with syllables, letters, and numbers. Call attention to the fact that minor songs usually begin and end on *la*.

4. Have the class sing the song with syllables, numbers, and letters.

5. Now sing two and three-part minor songs.

For an *harmonic minor* song follow much the same procedure, but point out that the seventh step is raised in both the scale and song.

KEY OF C MINOR (HARMONIC MINOR)

LA	TI	DO	RE	MI	FA	SI	LA
6	7	1	2	3	4	5	6
C	D	Eb	F	G	Ab	B♮	C

In presenting a *melodic minor* song explain that in the ascending melodic minor scale the sixth and seventh steps are raised a half step, but in the descending melodic minor those sixth and seventh steps are made natural, so that the descending scale becomes a normal minor.

KEY OF C MINOR (MELODIC MINOR)

LA	TI	DO	RE	MI	FI	SI	LA	LA	SOL	FA	MI	RE	DO	TI	LA
6	7	1	2	3	4	5	6	6	5	4	3	2	1	7	6
C	D	Eb	F	G	A♮	B♮	C	C	Bb	Ab	G	F	Eb	D	C

Suggest to the class that they write the three different kinds of minor scales.

TESTING VOICES. Voice testing may need to be done — particularly in the eighth grade. However, until their voices seem to settle into one category, rotate the boys and girls on their parts so that they will gain experience in singing both melody and harmony, both high and low music. Consult pages 99-103 for suggestions on voice testing.

MODULATION. Modulation is taught through the analysis of songs. The class will discover that in some songs there is melodic progression from one key to another but the songs always end in the original key.

STUDY OF THE BASIC FUNDAMENTALS. Fundamentals are necessary only as needed in singing a song, only as needed to enhance the appreciation of what is being done. The following fundamentals, *as they occur in songs,* should be taught:

> Major and Minor key signatures
> Meter signatures
> Bass Clef (if there are changing or changed voices in the group)
> Terms of expression

Sometimes classes spend so much time talking about the music that there is scarcely time left to *make* music. After a boy's voice has changed he will be glad to learn about the bass clef. Until then he has no need for that knowledge. How a student *feels* about what he knows is more important than *what* he knows.

SEATING ARRANGEMENTS. Seating a group heterogeneously is a much more acceptable practice than seating it according to ability. The advantages of having the good musicians at the back of the room are far overshadowed by the disadvantages of this arrangement. Front seats are a daily reminder to the less musical students that they do not measure up to the standard of the class.

Rhythm Activities

Young people with an adequate elementary music background will be able to take in their stride the rhythm problems encountered in their regular texts. Again, as in singing, those who had little opportunity earlier and those who were not able to grasp what was given them will need assistance in becoming rhythmically alert.

Rhythm is so much a part of young people, so inherent within them that they are usually eager to do anything and everything rhythmical. Sometimes their responses are chaotic and then it is the teacher's responsibility to guide those reactions into the proper channels.

A mathematical analysis of rhythm is often meaningless to a teen-ager. However, he usually knows how music makes him feel; he knows how he would like to respond and *that* he must be allowed to do. If he can feel the rhythm of the polka because he has been dancing the polka, if he can feel the skip music because he has been skipping, then, when he sees the symbols of these rhythms on the printed page, they will probably mean something to him.

Boys and girls enjoy square dancing and folk dancing. In the basic music texts a number of suggestions are given for dance steps and dance formations; these, by all means, should become a part of the music period. If the regular classroom is not large enough to permit dancing, perhaps an arrangement may be made for using the gymnasium or activity room; or, if that is not possible, a part of the group may participate in the classroom, even in a comparatively small area. Later the other members of the class may have their turn.

Encourage the students to make up their own dances. When once they know a variety of dance steps and fundamental rhythms, these can be combined into charming dances.

So many different rhythmic responses are possible. Practically every song will lend itself to a touch of rhythm activity. Keep rhythm instruments accessible so they can be used when needed. Drums used with Indian music, maracas and tambourines used with Latin-American music, shakers used with syncopated music, sticks used with martial music are all very appealing. Encourage the students to make their own instruments. A few suggestions from the teacher will lead to an interesting array of instruments. Stretching inner-tubing over tin cans, putting pebbles in gourds, striking two large nails together, and dozens of other such possibilities can be used.

Dalcrose Eurythmics, in addition to being fun, will rapidly develop strong rhythmic concepts. See page 5 for the discussion of this area of rhythm training.

It would seem unlikely that rhythm activities could be over-emphasized. If students can read the rhythm of a piece of music correctly, it is very possible that both the melody and harmony will fall into place for them rather naturally. Let the students clap, step, scan, and dance. They will have a delightful time and the teacher will have a good music group.

Experiences with Audio-Visual Aids

LISTENING TO RECORDINGS. In the past the term "music appreciation" was directly applicable only to listening to recordings. Some teachers called drilling on isolated facts music appreciation, but this does not guarantee appreciation. Certainly it is neither creative nor inspiring. Every music lesson must be a lesson in appreciation, and listening is only *one* means to that end.

Boys and girls should be given tools to make them more intelligent listeners. The music they listen to should be good. A teacher should show respect for his art by refusing to identify himself with that which is in poor taste musically.

All the while that listening goes on, other integrative areas should be given due consideration. The students should be encouraged to use various art media to illustrate what they are hearing. They might do finger painting while listening, make murals of a story, use rhythm instruments, do simple dramatizations, or, occasionally, hum while a record is being played. The possibilities are limitless.

Encourage the students to attend concerts. They will enjoy young people's concerts by visiting artists, church choir concerts, and concerts by performing groups from the schools (elementary, junior, and senior high schools).

There are fewer and fewer makers of music and more and more listeners to music. It is, therefore, our obligation to make those listeners intelligent and discriminating. Everything must be done to elevate the listening tastes of pupils.

USING FILMS. Films are listed within the various units. More and better films are increasingly available for school use. They should not be used indiscriminately, however. Give the students some background: tell them the story; make necessary explanations so that seeing a film is not just "busy work" but a meaningful experience. The following outline may serve as a guide for the presentation of all films:

How to Present A Film

Miracle on the Mesa

Year: Seventh

Objective: To stimulate an integrated study of music, art, crafts, and sciences in relation to the Hopi Indians.

The teachers of music, social studies, English, art, and physical education should work together in setting up the background for film presentations. In each student's notebook should be notes from reading references and class discussions covering the following items:

1. Physical aspects of the country in which the Hopi Indians live
2. Their living conditions
3. Their occupation
4. Their schools
5. Characteristics of the Hopi Indians

On the bulletin board there should be numerous pictures pertaining to the study. The students may write to Chambers of Commerce or to Indian Agencies in the southwestern states for descriptive material and pictures for the bulletin board.

On a display table there should be articles made by the Indians of the Southwest. Students may bring many of these items.

When this background is laid, present the film. The first

showing should be done without comment. Follow the film with a discussion after which:

1. Have the pupils bring native musical instruments.
2. Make some instruments which the Indians would use.
3. Learn the songs of the Hopi Indians.
4. Play records of Indian music and music which is based on themes from Indian folklore.
5. Learn some of the Indian dances.
6. Make some articles from clay.

Show the film again, this time stopping for discussion. Activities which could logically follow the showing of the film include:

1. Completion of notebooks.
2. A guest day where another seventh grade could be invited to the room to enjoy the display and to share the information the class has gained in the project. Brief talks, dances, singing, and the playing of instruments might be included. Make sure that every pupil has a part in this guest day.

LISTENING TO THE RADIO AND WATCHING TELEVISION. The teacher and pupils together should make an annotated list of radio and TV programs. Some of the broadcasts take place at the same time each week throughout the year. For special occasions there will be special broadcasts. Encourage the boys and girls to watch the Radio-TV section in the newspaper for suggestions. Reports on special broadcasts may be given in class and condensations of the reports may be put into the notebooks.

Creative Activities

It is important to encourage the students to create melodies. So much of this is done in elementary schools these days that junior high school students find it perfectly natural to compose. If boys and girls at this level have not had much previous experience in melody writing, the teacher can introduce it in several ways.

1. Use a poem which the class knows and likes; set it to music following these suggestions:

   a. Make the words fit the music and vice versa.

   b. While reading the poem, beat or clap the pulse.

   c. If possible, draw out the melody for the entire song. If it will not come this way, approach it line by line.

   d. Through their feeling for accent, question the class as to how it swings: in twos, threes, or fours.

   e. Have the class notate the song, a copy of which should go into their notebooks. Some of the group may wish to illustrate their songs.

2. Encourage the boys and girls to write poetry either in school or at home. Each unit ought to inspire an original poem or two, either directly or as an outgrowth of the unit. In setting an original poem to music, follow the suggestions outlined above.

3. Compose the words and music simultaneously.

4. Write a harmony part to a familiar melody. Any group with considerable experience in writing one-part melodies and in part singing can do this easily. This will point up range and simple theory to the group.

5. Make up new words to a familiar song for adaptation to a particular unit.

6. When several melodies have been written, combine them into a dramatization or into a simple operetta or pageant.

7. Write rounds. This will go farther toward an understanding of the canon and fugue style of writing than any amount of talking about it.

8. Write descants. Using a simple song like "Row Your Boat", the teacher may suggest any one or a combination of the following easy descants:

ROW YOUR BOAT

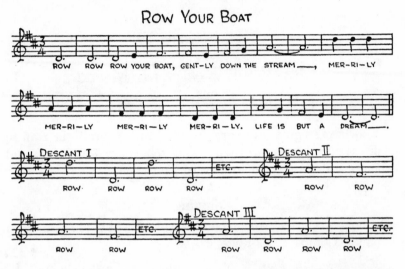

9. Following this, sing other songs such as "London Bridge", "Swing Low Sweet Chariot", "Are You Sleeping?" and encourage the students to make their own descants. When they are able to do this, they will see possibilities for descants in many of the songs which they sing.

10. Write the piano accompaniment or chording for the piano, ukulele, and autoharp for original songs or for songs that are being sung in class.

Neither students nor teachers are aware of how much learning is really going on in these various creative activities. The learning is subtle, but it is there nevertheless. The student will need to know how many sharps or flats must go into the signature if the home tone is on the first line. He will need to know he must use a slow note on a long word. When he realizes he needs to know some basic fundamentals, he will be perfectly willing to learn them.

UNIT I (Grade VII)

Our Way West with Music

Folk Music in Westward Expansion

Cowboys singing on the range, the Santa Fe trail, the trail to
Old Mexico, great open spaces as related to folk songs and
dances will be of great interest to study.

Singing

Bridgman, Curtis. THE AMERICAN SINGER BOOK VII. American
Book Company, Chicago, 1947.

Goodbye, Old Paint	American Cowboy	
	Ballad	Page 11

Wilson, Leeder, Gee. MUSIC AMERICANS SING. Silver Burdett
Company, Chicago, 1948.

Old Joe Clark		Page 84
On Top of Old Smoky	Mountain Ballad	Page 74
Out Among the Redmen	English	Page 24

McConathy, Beattie, Morgan. MUSIC HIGHWAYS AND BYWAYS.
Silver Burdett Company, Chicago, 1936.

Dying Cowboy, The	Cowboy Ballad	Page 78
Little Joe the Wrangler	Cowboy Ballad	Page 84
Trail to Mexico, The	Cowboy Ballad	Page 80
Zebra Dun, The	Cowboy Ballad	Page 82

Dykema, Pitcher, Stevens, Vandevere. MUSIC IN THE AIR. C. C.
Birchard and Company, Boston, 1947.

Night Herding Song	Cowboy Song	Page 29

McConathy, Beattie, Morgan. MUSIC OF MANY LANDS AND PEO-
PLES. Silver Burdett Company, Chicago, 1932.

Santa Fe Trail	Traditional	Page 99

16

Texas Cowboy's
    Stampede Song   Traditional   Page 98

Wilson, Leeder, Gee, Greer. MUSIC THE WORLD SINGS. Silver
Burdett Company, Chicago, 1952.
   Prairie Waltz   Reynolds   Page 136

Dykema, Pitcher, Stevens, Vandevere. SING OUT! C. C. Birchard
and Company, Boston, 1946.
   Dogie Song   Cowboy Song   Page 150
   Home on the Range   Cowboy Song   Page 148
   Song of the "Lone Prairee" McKay   Page 23

Glenn, Leavitt, Rebmann, Baker. TREASURE. Ginn and Company, Chicago, 1938.
   Oh, Saddle the Roan   Bauer   Page 126

Rhythm Activities

From SING OUT! learn the songs and the dance steps on pages
28-37; then use these same dance steps on other songs.

On page 41 of MUSIC AMERICANS SING are square dance directions. Do the dance as suggested.

On pages 244, 245 of MUSIC HIGHWAYS AND BYWAYS will be
found square dance directions.

While singing a song ("Home on the Range" for instance) pre-
tend to throw a lasso in time to the music, use rhythm sticks
and hollowed-out coconuts to imitate the sound of the horse's
hoofs, etc.

Create dances and dance formations.

Use the recording LET'S DANCE THE SQUARE DANCE for square
dancing.

Audio-Visual Aids

1. Recordings
   Big Rock Candy Mountain
   Early American Ballads, sung by John Jacob Niles

Home on the Range, sung by John Charles Thomas
Let's Go to the Rodeo
Rodeo, Four Dance Episodes (Aaron Copland)
Square Dances, performed by Woodhull's Masters

2. Films

BROKEN ARROW.   Films Incorporated.
The Westward Movement from the Indians' point of view.

BUFFALO BILL RIDES AGAIN.   Films Incorporated.
This is both educational and historical.

PROMENADE ALL.   MENC Handbook.
This shows a wide variety of square dances made in cooperation with the Folk Dancing Federation of California.

TO HEAR THE BANJO PLAY.   MENC Handbook.
This shows folk song and dance in the lives of people of the present as well as the past.

Supplementary Films:

AMERICAN COWBOY, THE.	Ford Films.
AMERICAN SQUARE DANCES.	MENC Handbook.
BALLADS OF THE PLAINS.	Bell and Howell Company.
BUCKSKIN FRONTIER.	Films Incorporated.
BUFFALO BILL.	Films Incorporated.
COMMUNICATIONS WESTWARD.	Teaching Film Custodians, Inc.
HEN HOP.	MENC Handbook.
LAST DOGIE.	Wm. M. Dennis Film Libraries.
MOZART AND BARRIOS ON SIX STRINGS (guitar).	MENC Handbook.
PIONEERS OF THE PLAINS.	Encyclopaedia Britannica Films, Inc.
SONGS OF THE RANGE.	Bell and Howell Company.
WESTWARD MOVEMENT.	Encyclopaedia Britannica Films, Inc.

3. Other Visual Aids

Present an opportunity for the students to become familiar with the paintings of Charles Russell and other western artists. Have the students trace on individual maps the more important historical trails to the West. (This activity could be enlarged to include a mural on the blackboard or bulletin board.)

Creative Activities

In addition to making up dances, write some original songs. This may be done by using a well-known poem and setting it to music or making up both the words and the tune. A simple operetta might emerge from combining several tunes. Writing descants for a well-known tune and adding a second part to a melody are other creative possibilities.

Other Activities

Learn the meanings of terms and words peculiar to the cowboy language.

Determine the distinction between commercial cowboy music (movie cowboys) and true cowboy music.

Learn the I IV V_7 chords by sight and sound. Having learned them, use them for piano chording, for playing the guitar, the ukulele, and the autoharp.

References for learning these instruments are:

Autoharp Accompaniments to Old Favorite Songs (Manual of Instructions), Lillian Mohr Fox, C. C. Birchard and Company, Boston, 1947.

Handbook for Teaching Piano Classes, MENC, 64 East Jackson Boulevard, Chicago 4, Illinois.

Depressles Guitar Method, Rubank, Incorporated, Chicago, Illinois.

Method for The Recorder, by Giesbert, Associated Music Publishers, Incorporated, N.Y.

800 Years of Music for Recorders, edited by A. Hess, Associated Music Publishers, Incorporated, N.Y.

Songs from Everywhere, The Song Flute Co., 630 S. Wabash Avenue, Chicago, Illinois.

Game of Music Building, Book II, by N. Owen, The Song Flute Company, 630 S. Wabash Avenue, Chicago, Illinois.

Tonette Tunes and Technique, by H. Davis, Rubank, Incorporated, Chicago, Illinois.

Keep a notebook of appropriate pictures (original and clipped from magazines), favorite ballads, and notes from class reports.

Music Reading Assignments

Lomax, John A. and Alan. AMERICAN BALLADS AND FOLK SONGS. The Macmillan Company, New York, 1934.

Cowboy Songs   Page 375

Sandburg, Carl. THE AMERICAN SONGBAG. Harcourt, Brace and Company, New York, 1927.

Great Open Spaces, The   Page 259

Luther, Frank. AMERICANS AND THEIR SONGS. Harper and Brothers, New York, 1942.

Cowboy Songs   Page 193

Society for Curriculum Study Incorporated. BUILDING AMERICA, VOLUME VII, NO. 8 (Periodical). New York, 1942.

Lomax, John A. and Alan. COWBOY SONGS. The Macmillan Company, New York, 1946.

Cowboy Songs and Other Frontier Ballads   Page   4

Lomax, John A. and Alan. FOLK SONGS U. S. A. The Macmillan Company, New York, 1948.

Git Along, Little Dogies   Page 192

Ford, Mr. and Mrs. Henry. GOOD MORNING. Dearborn, Michigan, 1943.

Music Calls and Directions for Old Time Dancing

KEYBOARD JUNIOR. 1346 Chapel Street, New Haven 11, Connecticut.

Boots and Saddles	Volume IV, No. 4,		
	January, 1946	Page	3
Whole World Plays the	Volume X, No. 6,		
Guitar, The	March, 1952	Page	6

Stringham, Edwin John. LISTENING TO MUSIC CREATIVELY. Prentice-Hall, Incorporated, New York, 1946.

Folk Song, The	Page 28

Gee, Leeder, Wilson. LOG FOR MUSIC AMERICANS SING. Silver Burdett Company, New York, 1949.

Over Mountain, River, and Plain	Page 46

McKinney, Howard D. MUSIC AND MAN. American Book Company, New York, 1948.

Sing Out, Sweet Land	Chapter III

Kinscella, Hazel G. MUSIC AND ROMANCE. RCA Victor Company, Camden, New Jersey, 1930.

American Music on Its Way	Page 338

McConathy, Beattie, Morgan. MUSIC HIGHWAYS AND BYWAYS. Silver Burdett Company, Chicago, 1936.

Songs the Cowboys Sing	Page 76

Siegmeister, Eli (Edited by). THE MUSIC LOVER'S HANDBOOK. William Morrow and Company, New York, 1943.

Fiddle Strings and Ballads	Page 17
Nature and Evolution of Folk Song, The	Page 33
Past and Future of Folk Music, The	Page 47
Some Reflections on Folk Song	Page 37

McConathy, Beattie, Morgan. MUSIC OF MANY LANDS AND PEOPLES. Silver Burdett Company, Chicago, 1932.

Frontier Days	Page 94

Bauer, Peyser. MUSIC THROUGH THE AGES. G. P. Putnam's Sons, New York, 1932.

Cowboy on the Plains   Page 397

Lomax, John A. and Alan. OUR SINGING COUNTRY. The Macmillan Company, New York, 1941.

Cowboy Songs   Page 236
Outlaws   Page 303

UNIT II (Grade VII)

Music in Colonial Life

*Culture in the New World, a Reflection of the
Mother Countries*

The songs, dances, and customs of very early America as
compared with those of Continental Europe and of Mozart's
time are interesting to study and observe.

Singing

McConathy et al. AMERICAN MUSIC HORIZONS. Silver Burdett
Company, Chicago, 1951.

How Cavaliers Have Changed	Mozart	Page 160

Bridgman, Curtis. THE AMERICAN SINGER BOOK VII. American
Book Company, Chicago, 1947.

Washington's Birthday	Boynton	Page 213

Wilson, Leeder, Gee. MUSIC AMERICANS SING. Silver Burdett
Company, Chicago, 1948.

Constitution and the Guerriere, The	1812 Ballad	Page 37
Hey Betty Martin	American Traditional	Page 33
Riflemen's Song at Bennington	Allison	Page 36

McConathy, Beattie, Morgan. MUSIC OF MANY LANDS AND PEO-
PLE. Silver Burdett Company, Chicago, 1932.

Contentment	Mozart	Page 25
Landing of the Pilgrims	Browne	Page 90
Old Hundred	Psalter	Page 89

23

Wilson, Leeder, Gee, Greer. MUSIC THE WORLD SINGS. Silver Burdett Company, Chicago, 1952.

Hymn of the Pilgrims	MacDowell	Page 14

Glenn, Leavitt, Rebmann. SING ALONG. Ginn and Company, Chicago, 1941.

By Golden Chains	Mozart	Page 73
Land of Youth, The	Mozart	Page 133
Sweet Betsy from Pike	Traditional	Page 28

Dykema, Pitcher, Stevens, Vandevere. SING OUT! C. C. Birchard and Company, Boston, 1946.

Alphabet, The	Mozart	Page 232
Barbara Allen	Virginia Ballad	Page 39
Captain Jinks	Old American Song	Page 32
Chester	Billings	Page 16
Concord Hymn	Clokey	Page 14
Cumberland Gap	Early American Song	Page 43
Jiffery, James and John	Vermont Folk Song	Page 42
Jolly Old Roger	Vermont Folk Song	Page 41
Valley Forge	Vandevere	Page 15
Yankee Doodle	American Song	Page 18

Glenn, Leavitt, Rebmann. TREASURE. Ginn and Company, Chicago, 1938.

All Wise Nature	Mozart	Page 9
Carpenter, The	American Traditional	Page 28
Frog in the Spring	American Traditional	Page 60
Green Willow	American Traditional	Page 41
Rosy Boy, Posy Boy	American Traditional	Page 12
What Is This Splendor	Mozart	Page 155

Rhythm Activities

Learn the minuet. If the boys do not enjoy doing this rather stately type of dance, they may choose to form a fife and drum corps as suggested on page 33 of MUSIC AMERICANS SING.

Make up a dance (the Virginia Reel lends itself well) to

Captain Jinks, or follow the directions on page 26 of SING OUT! Choose any other of the dances on pages 28-37 of SING OUT! to learn and enjoy.

Make up a dance for *Frog in the Spring,* page 60 of TREASURE. Occasionally, do Dalcroze movements on song materials.

Audio-Visual Aids

1. Recordings

Early American Ballads, sung by John Jacob Niles
March of the Priests from "The Magic Flute" (Mozart)
Marriage of Figaro—Overture (Mozart)
Minuet from Divertimento (Mozart-Heifetz), performed by Heifetz
Minuet from "Don Giovanni" (Mozart)
Quartet No. 15 in D Minor (Mozart)
Rounds and Jingles, by the King's Men
Said the Piano to the Harpsichord
Sonata No. 8 in C (Mozart)
Symphony No. 41—Jupiter (Mozart)
Turkish March (Mozart), played on the harpsichord by Wanda Landowska

2. Films

COLONIAL WILLIAMSBURG.   MENC Handbook.
This shows town life, customs, costumes and the music of the period.

EINE KLEINE NACHTMUSIK.   MENC Handbook.
Mozart's lovely serenade, "A Little Night Music", is played by the Vienna Symphony Orchestra with Krips conducting.

HARPSICHORD, THE.   MENC Handbook.
Lovely music was written for this instrument (which is the forerunner of the piano) by Bach, Handel, William Byrd, Mozart, and others. Its tones are heard in this film which shows both the beauty of appearance and the physical structure of the harpsichord.

MARRIAGE OF FIGARO, THE.   Brandon Films, Inc.

This Mozart opera is brought admirably to the screen. The perfection of Mozart's music has in no way been sacrificed to the visual presentation of this comedy plot. The performance of the Berlin State Orchestra is excellent.

Supplementary Films:

COLONIAL CHILDREN.	Encyclopaedia Britannica Films, Inc.
DOLMETSCH FAMILY, THE.	MENC Handbook.
IN MOZART'S FOOTSTEPS.	Brandon Films, Inc.
MOUNT VERNON.	Eastin Films, Inc.
MOZART AND BARRIOS ON SIX STRINGS.	MENC Handbook.
TEN MINUETS WITH MOZART.	Ideal Pictures Corporation.
WASHINGTON IN VIRGINIA.	Eastin Pictures, Inc.

3. Other Visual Aids

Study portrait paintings of the 18th Century (Gainsborough, Reynolds, Goya, and others).

Study the architecture of Colonial America and 18th Century Europe.

Chalk illustrations of scenes of this period may be made.

Creative Activities

Make up songs about this period.

Make drums for a drum corps.

After learning the minuet and the Virginia Reel, adapt these dances to several songs. Design simple costumes or touches of costuming to go along with the dances.

Other Activities

Other related areas of the period that might be developed, if interest and time permit, concern these people:

Literature and Statesmen:
Benjamin Franklin
Patrick Henry
Alexander Hamilton
Thomas Jefferson

Inventors:
James Watt, inventor of the steam engine.
Benjamin Franklin, electrical research.
Eli Whitney, inventor of the cotton gin.
James Hargreaves, inventor of the spinning-jenny.
Elias Howe, inventor of the sewing-machine.
Cyrus H. McCormick, inventor of the reaping-machine.

A similar development of related areas may be done for the Nineteenth Century using the following individuals of that period:

Historian:
Francis Parkman

Orators:
Henry Clay
Daniel Webster

Writers of fiction:
James Fenimore Cooper
Nathaniel Hawthorne
Washington Irving

Essayists:
Ralph Waldo Emerson
Oliver Wendell Holmes
Henry D. Thoreau

Poets:
William Cullen Bryant
Henry W. Longfellow
James Russell Lowell
Edgar Allen Poe
Walt Whitman
John Greenleaf Whittier

The students may wish to make dioramas of some phase of colonial life. Directions for making a diorama are as follows:

Use a box (the size to be determined by the needs of the particular project). Turn the open side frontwards. Have the students design the background which will line the two sides and the back of the box. Select the necessary figures which will illustrate the subject. The three dimensional effect is produced by the correct placement of the figures, near or away from the background. It is quite possible to gain satisfactory results without lighting, but proper lighting adds greatly to the desired effect. Lighting may be from above or below.

Music Reading Assignments

GOOD HOUSEKEEPING MAGAZINE. The Hearst Corporation, 57th Street at 8th Avenue, New York. February, 1952.

Mozart Mystery, The	Page 123

Schwimmer, Franciska. GREAT MUSICIANS AS CHILDREN. Doubleday, Doran and Company, Garden City, New York, 1929.

Taming the Customs Guard	Page 20

Spaeth, Sigmund. A HISTORY OF POPULAR MUSIC IN AMERICA. Garden City Publishing Company, Incorporated, Garden City, New York, 1948.

Round Our Infancy	Page 15
Stirring Sixties, The	Page 137

Bauer, Peyser. HOW MUSIC GREW. G. P. Putnam's Sons, New York, 1925.

Characteristics of Mozart's Music	Page 137
Clavier, The	Page 141
Harpsichord, The	Page 310
Mozart's Dramatic Music	Page 139
Overture to the "Magic Flute"	Page 140
Viennese School, The—Mozart	Page 134

Kent, Tarshis. IN GOOD OLD COLONIAL TIMES. Riverside Press, Cambridge, Massachusetts, 1941.

Music Societies	Page 38

Bernstein, Martin. INTRODUCTION TO MUSIC. Prentice-Hall, Incorporated, New York, 1937.

Wolfgang Amadeus Mozart	Page 134

Jones, Barnard. INTRODUCTION TO MUSICAL KNOWLEDGE. Paul A. Schmitt Music Company, Minneapolis, Minnesota, 1935.

Early Instruments—The Harpsichord   Page 51
Mozart   Page 135

Kinscella, Hazel G. KINSCELLA READER, BOOK V. The University
Publishing Company, Chicago, 1927.

King and the Magic Stick, The   Page 353
Little Magician of Music, The   Page 174
Mount Vernon Bells   Page 341
Music with Reed Pipes   Page 1

Kinscella, Hazel G. KINSCELLA READER, BOOK VI. The University
Publishing Company, Chicago, 1929.

Magic Flute, The   Page 51
Mozart's Surprise   Page 140
Story of the Keyboard, The   Page 213

Baldwin, Lillian. A LISTENER'S ANTHOLOGY OF MUSIC, VOLUME 1.
Silver Burdett Company, Chicago, 1948.

Artist, The   Page 110
Magic Flute, The (Overture)   Page 118
Marriage of Figaro, The (Overture)   Page 116
Mozart Mirrors the Eighteenth Century   Chapter IV

Bolton, Sarah K. LIVES OF POOR BOYS WHO BECAME FAMOUS.
Thomas Y. Crowell Company, New York, 1947.

Wolfgang Amadeus Mozart   Page 36

Gee, Leeder, Wilson. LOG FOR MUSIC AMERICANS SING. Silver
Burdett Company, Chicago, 1949.

Musket, Fife and Drum   Page 16

Lawrence, Robert. THE MAGIC FLUTE. Artists and Writers
Guild, Incorporated, New York, 1944.

Kinscella, Hazel G. MUSIC AND ROMANCE. RCA Victor Company, Camden, New Jersey, 1930.

Harpsichord, The   Page 287
Mozart   Pages 353, 457

Siegmeister, Eli (Edited by). THE MUSIC LOVER'S HANDBOOK. William Morrow and Company, New York, 1943.

Mozart	Page 395
Music in Early America	Page 661
Prefaces to "The New England Psalm Singer" and	
"The Singing Master's Assistant"	Page 662
Wolfgang Amadeus Mozart (Jupiter Symphony)	Page 152

Howard, John Tasker. MUSIC OF GEORGE WASHINGTON'S TIME. United States - George Washington Bi-Centennial Commission, Washington Building, Washington, D.C., 1931.

Music Associated with Historic Events	Page 9
Music Issued by Music Publishers	Page 24
Musical Background, The	Page 5

Bacon, Mrs. Mary S. OPERAS EVERY CHILD SHOULD KNOW. Grosset and Dunlap, New York, 1911.

Magic Flute, The	Chapter X

Hartshorn, Leavitt. THE PILOT. (Making Friends with Music). Ginn and Company, Chicago, 1940.

Four German Dances	Page 35
Minuet from Symphony in D Major	Page 110
Overture to "The Marriage of Figaro"	Page 85

Hartshorn, Leavitt. PRELUDE. (Making Friends with Music). Ginn and Company, Chicago, 1940.

Four German Dances	Page 37
Overture to "The Marriage of Figaro"	Page 119

Hartshorn, Leavitt. PROGRESS. (Making Friends with Music). Ginn and Company, Chicago, 1940.

Minuet from Symphony in D Major	Page 25

Spaeth, Sigmund. STORIES BEHIND THE WORLD'S GREAT MUSIC. Garden City Publishing Company, Incorporated, Garden City, New York, 1937.

Mozart Writes His Own Requiem	Page 67

Lyons, John Henry. STORIES OF OUR AMERICAN PATRIOTIC SONGS. The Vanguard Press, New York, 1942.

Two Patriotic Marches   Page 23

Barbour, Freeman. STORY OF MUSIC. C. C. Birchard and Company, Boston, 1938.

Mozart   Page 73

Enjoying Animals and Nature through Music

Relating Things about Us to Music

The graceful movements of a swan, the fury of an approaching storm, the calmness of a flowing river become more meaningful through musical expression.

Singing

Bridgman, Curtis. THE AMERICAN SINGER BOOK VIII. American Book Company, Chicago, 1947.

Fog	Bridgman	Page 71
Sea Gulls, The	Early California Song	Page 146
Skiing	Holman	Page 116

Bridgman, Curtis. THE AMERICAN SINGER BOOK VIII. American Book Company, Chicago, 1948.

Leaves in the Fall	Old Folk Tune	Page 14
Old Dog Tray	Foster	Page 172
Yodeling Parakeet	Curtis	Page 12

Wilson, Leeder, Gee. MUSIC AMERICANS SING. Silver Burdett Company, Chicago, 1948.

America the Beautiful	Ward	Page 94
Animal Fair, The	College Song	Page 16
Down the River	Old Chantey	Page 78

McConathy, Beattie, Morgan. MUSIC HIGHWAYS AND BYWAYS. Silver Burdett Company, Chicago, 1936.

Kites Are Flying	Chinese Folk Song	Page 210
Spring	Swedish Folk Song	Page 8

Wilson, Leeder, Gee, Greer. MUSIC THE WORLD SINGS. Silver Burdett Company, Chicago, 1952.

Goat, The	Cooper	Page 9

Dykema, Pitcher, Stevens, Vandevere. SING OUT! C. C. Birchard and Company, Boston, 1946.

Barnyard Glee Club, The	French Folk Tune	Page 177
Bees	Davis	Page 237
Bird, The	Rubinstein	Page 202
Butterflies	Schumann	Page 198
Climate, The	Old Melody	Page 176
Fireflies	McKay	Page 211
Old MacDonald Had a Farm	Templeton	Page 180
Seein' the Elephant	Forty-niners' Song	Page 154

Glenn, Leavitt, Rebmann. TREASURE. Ginn and Company, Chicago, 1938.

Indian Summer	Golde	Page 48
Robin in the Rain, The	English	Page 144
White Butterflies	Nelson	Page 184

Rhythm Activities

While singing "Old MacDonald Had a Farm" (SING OUT!, page 181) divide the group into different kinds of animals (pig, cow, duck, etc.). As the name of each animal is sung, have that group stand and imitate the animal.

In this connection another good rhythm activity is to have a barnyard chorus. Divide the group into the following animal classifications:

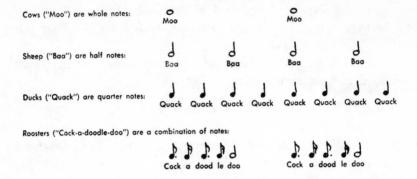

Using this as a round the cows "moo" for two measures, then the sheep enter, followed by ducks and roosters. While the boys and girls clap their rhythm, they chant their animal call. Rhythm instruments also may be used; for instance, cows may use triangles, sheep may use sticks, ducks may use shakers or maracas. Let the students suggest which instruments to use on the various parts.

Do Dalcroze movements on such songs as "America the Beautiful."

Audio-Visual Aids

1. Recordings

   America the Beautiful (Ward)
   Animal Fair
   Carnival of Animals (Saint-Saëns)
   Flight of the Bumble Bee (Rimsky-Korsakoff)
   Papillons, No. 8 (Schumann)
   Prelude to the Afternoon of a Faun (Debussy)
   Skater's Waltz (Waldteufel)
   Spring Song (Mendelssohn)
   Storm from William Tell Overture, The (Rossini)
   Swan of Tuonela (Sibelius)
   Wild Horsemen, The (Schumann)

2. Films

AMERICA THE BEAUTIFUL.   MENC Handbook.
The words and music of this song evoke a mood suited
to a visual pageant which shows the beauty and strength
of this mighty land of ours.

ANIMAL FAIR, THE.   Teaching Film Custodians, Inc.
Glimpses are seen of many unusual and little-known
animals from over the world.

CHILDREN'S CORNER SUITE.   MENC Handbook.
Alfred Cortot is heard playing "The Children's Corner", a suite of pieces for piano by Debussy. This music
provides the background for a pictorial fantasy of ani-
mated type.

HEN HOP.   MENC Handbook.
This is an amusing hand-drawn pictorial fantasy suggested by folk music of the country dance type. Simple
geometric forms build up rhythmically into the shape
of a hen. An egg with two feet joins the hen in dancing
old-time jigs, waltzes, and reels of the barn dance type.

Supplementary Films:

ANIMALS IN WINTER.   Encyclopaedia Britannica
                            Films, Inc.

ANTS.   Encyclopaedia Britannica
                            Films, Inc.

BEAUTY AND THE BLADE.   Teaching Film
                            Custodians, Inc.

BIRDS ARE INTERESTING.   Encyclopaedia Britannica
                            Films, Inc.

BIRTH OF THE SOIL—PART I.   Encyclopaedia Britannica
                            Films, Inc.

BUTTERFLIES.   Encyclopaedia Britannica
                            Films, Inc.

FLOWERS AT WORK.   Encyclopaedia Britannica
                            Films, Inc.

HONEYLAND.	Teaching Film Custodians, Inc.
LOON'S NECKLACE, THE.	MENC Handbook.
NATURE'S BALLET.	MENC Handbook.
OUR EARTH.	Encyclopaedia Britannica Films, Inc.
PAULETTE, GRISE, LA.	MENC Handbook.
RIVER, THE.	MENC Handbook.
SKIING IS BELIEVING.	Teaching Film Custodians, Inc.
ZOO.	Encyclopaedia Britannica Films, Inc.

3. Other Visual Aids.

Illustrations of animals may be made. A mural of the "Carnival of Animals" may be done.

Landscape paintings by Cezanné and other artists may be studied.

Creative Activities

Make up poems and songs about animals, nature, and weather. If there are a number of songs about several animals, an animal fair can be held in class.

Make up descants for "America the Beautiful" and "Old Mac-Donald." Learn the chords for these songs and play them on the ukulele, autoharp, and piano.

Other Activities

Put illustrations of animals in notebooks. Include a section on favorite stories and poems, original songs, and notes from class projects.

Music Reading Assignments

Bernstein, Martin. INTRODUCTION TO MUSIC. Prentice-Hall, Incorporated, New York, 1937.

Carnaval	Page 224
Robert Schumann	Page 219

KEYBOARD JUNIOR. 1346 Chapel Street, New Haven 11, Connecticut.

Camille Saint-Saëns
    Volume   7, No. 5, February, 1949   Page 1
Clair de Lune
    Volume 10, No. 5, February, 1952   Page 1
Clouds-Sea-Moonlight
    Volume 10, No. 5, February, 1952   Page 2
Edward MacDowell
    Volume   4, No. 3, December, 1945   (entire issue)
Golliwog's Cakewalk
    Volume 10, No. 5, February, 1952   Page 6
Handel's Water Music
    Volume   8, No. 1, October, 1949   Page 7
Insect Chorus, The
    Volume   7, No. 8, May, 1949   Page 1
Robert Schumann
    Volume   6, No. 1, October, 1947   (entire issue)
Spring Songs
    Volume   7, No. 6, March, 1949   Page 1
Swan, The
    Volume   7, No. 5, February, 1949   Page 6
To Spring
    Volume   8, No. 7, April, 1950   Page 1
Tone Poem
    Volume   7, No. 5, February, 1949   Page 5

Gee, Leeder, Wilson. LOG FOR MUSIC AMERICANS SING. Silver Burdett Company, Chicago, 1949.

America the Beautiful   Page 54

Kinscella, Hazel G. MUSIC AND ROMANCE. RCA Victor Company, Camden, New Jersey, 1930.

Adventures in a Perambulator   Page 520
Carnival of the Animals   Page 280
Children's Corner Suite   Page 208
Dancing Doll   Page 277
Flight of the Bumble Bee, The   Page 306
Golliwog's Cakewalk   Page 85
Hark, Hark the Lark   Page 98
Nightingale, The   Page 99
Nutcracker Ballet, The   Page 175
On Hearing the First Cuckoo in Spring   Page 214
Robert Schumann   Page 295
Waltz of the Flowers, The   Page 178
William Tell Overture   Page 389
Woodland Sketches   Page 377

Barbour, Freeman. STORY OF MUSIC. C. C. Birchard and Company, Boston, 1938.

Carnival of the Animals   Page 164
Hark, Hark the Lark (Schubert)   Page 111
To a Wild Rose and To a Water Lily (MacDowell) Page 261
Water Music, The (Handel)   Page 49

Music and Religion

Worship through Music

Through music can be expressed hopes, joys, fears, uncertainties. Of all the ways in which one can worship, music is one of the most satisfying experiences—"O sing unto the Lord a new song!"

Singing

McConathy et al. AMERICAN MUSIC HORIZONS. Silver Burdett Company, Chicago, 1951.

Lift Thine Eyes	Mendelssohn	Page 225
Lord, Dismiss Us with Thy Blessing	Italian	Page 62

Bridgman, Curtis. THE AMERICAN SINGER BOOK VII. American Book Company, Chicago, 1947.

√ *God of Our Fathers*	Warren	Page 219
Holy, Holy, Holy	Dykes	Page 218
Lord God of Morning	Beethoven	Page 218
√ *Oh, Worship the King*	Haydn	Page 220
√ *Vesper Hymn, The*	Bortnianski	Page 26

Dykema, Pitcher, Vandevere. LET MUSIC RING! C. C. Birchard and Company, Boston, 1949.

Alleluia	Bryce	Page 96
√ *Lord My Pasture Shall Prepare, The*	Shaw	Page 97
Prayer	Frieswyck	Page 97
√ *Sanctus*	Schubert	Page 96

Wilson, Leeder, Gee. MUSIC AMERICANS SING. Silver Burdett
Company, Chicago, 1948.

All Praise to Thee	Tallis	Page 31
Fairest Lord Jesus	Silesian Folk Song	Page 103
Lord, Lord, You've Been		
So Good to Me	Kentucky	Page 99
Now the Day Is Over	Barnby	Page 103

McConathy, Beattie, Morgan. MUSIC HIGHWAYS AND BYWAYS.
Silver Burdett Company, Chicago, 1936.

Glorious Things of Thee		
Are Spoken	Haydn	Page 70
Morning Praise	Beethoven	Page 2
O Savior Sweet	Bach	Page 65

Wilson, Leeder, Gee, Greer. MUSIC THE WORLD SINGS. Silver
Burdett Company, Chicago, 1952.

Ave Maria	Schubert	Page 112
Intercessory Hymn	German	Page 20
Jesu, Joy of Man's Desiring	Bach	Page 118
O Come, O Come,		
Emmanuel	Gregorian	Page 36
O Rest in the Lord	Mendelssohn	Page 115

Dykema, Pitcher, Stevens, Vandevere. SING OUT! C. C. Birchard
and Company, Boston, 1946.

Break Forth, O Beauteous		
Heavenly Light	Bach	Page 192
Eternal Father Strong		
to Save	Dykes	Page 142
Faith of Our Fathers	Walton	Page 139
Father Hear Thy		
Children's Praises	Gotha-1715	Page 132
For the Beauty of the Earth	Kocher	Page 164
O Lord Most Holy	Franck	Page 140
Sing to the Lord	Gibb	Page 145

Glenn, Leavitt, Rebmann. SONG PARADE. Ginn and Company,
Chicago, 1941.

Prayer at Morning, A	Handel	Page 133
To God on High	Mendelssohn	Page 66
To Him from Whom Our		
Blessings Flow	Rossini	Page 117

Rhythm Activities

A rather new but very effective activity is rhythm movement to sacred songs. Compositions like "The Lord's Prayer", "Ave Maria", "The Holy City" can be used. For instructions and suggestions consult the book, THE ART OF THE RHYTHMIC CHOIR, Fisk.

As an added aid toward building strong rhythm concepts, the boys and girls should be taught to conduct the more simple meters as follows:

Four-Beat Measure

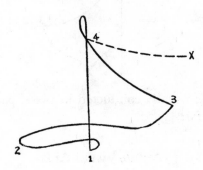

Three-Beat Measure

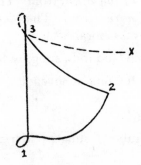

Two-Beat Measure

Six-Beat Measure

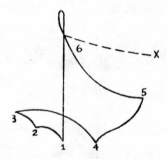

Six-eight time is usually conducted in two's, particularly when the rhythm is fast.

Audio-Visual Aids

1. Recordings

And the Glory of the Lord, from "The Messiah" (Handel)
Hallelujah Chorus, from "The Messiah" (Handel), sung by the Royal Choral Society

Ave Maria (Bach-Gounod), sung by Rosa Ponselle

Ave Maria (Bach-Gounod-Shvedoff), sung by the Don Cossacks
Hospodipomilui

Ave Maria (Schubert), sung by Marian Anderson

Children of the Heavenly Father, sung by the Augustana
Choir

Our Father, Merciful and Good

Holy City, The, by Fred Waring and His Pennsylvanians

Lord's Prayer, The, sung by de Paur's Infantry Chorus
Adoramus Te
O Bone Jesu

Lord's Prayer, The, by Fred Waring and His Pennsylvanians

My God and I, sung by the Latvian Singers

Songs of Devotion, by Fred Waring and His Pennsylvanians

Songs of Faith, sung by the Waring Chapel Choir

Who So Will Suffer God to Guide Him, sung by the
Trapp Family Choir

2. Films

CRUCIFIXION:THEME AND VARIATIONS.   MENC Handbook.
Musical arrangements of Verdi's "Requiem" and the
"Suites for Unaccompanied 'Cello" by Bach supply the
musical score. The pictorial theme of the Crucifixion
is shown in the works of three painters of the Middle
Ages.

EARTH SINGS, THE.   MENC Handbook.
This film, exceptional in both music and photography,
is composed of seven Palestinian folk songs illustrated
and interpreted by scores from pastoral Israel.

IMAGES MEDIEVALES.   MENC Handbook.
This is an art film using illuminated manuscripts to
give a picture of life in the Middle Ages. The musical
score by Guy Bernard makes use of music of the Medie-
val Period which is recorded with authentic instruments.

ONE GOD.   MENC Handbook.
This is a film based on Mary Fitch's book, "Music and
Religion". Its theme is the integral part played by music

in Jewish, Roman Catholic, Protestant, and other religious services and rituals.

Supplementary films:

AVE MARIA (Schubert), sung by Elizabeth Schumann.	Films Incorporated.
AVE MARIA (Bach-Gounod), sung by Jennie Tourel.	MENC Handbook.
AVE MARIA (Bach-Gounod), organ performance.	MENC Handbook.
CRUSADES.	Teaching Film Custodians, Inc.
DIE STEINERNEN WUNDER VON NAUMBERG.	MENC Handbook.
EILI, EILI.	MENC Handbook.
EULA BEAL.	MENC Handbook.
GEORGE FREDERICK HANDEL.	MENC Handbook.
HYMN OF THE NATIONS.	MENC Handbook.
LORD'S PRAYER, THE.	MENC Handbook.
MUSIC AND ARCHITECTURE THROUGH THE AGES.	MENC Handbook.
SINGING PIPES OR MUSIC IN THE WIND.	MENC Handbook.
SYMPHONIES IN STONE.	MENC Handbook.
THIS IS OUR EARTH.	MENC Handbook.
THREE PAINTINGS BY HIERONYMUS BOSCH.	MENC Handbook
YEHUDI MENUHIN.	MENC Handbook.

3. Other Visual Aids

Study the architecture of the cathedrals of the Gothic and Renaissance Periods.

Study the religious paintings of those periods.

Post on the bulletin board picture units on the development of the organ and of the bells.

Creative Activities

To the unison songs add second and/or third harmony parts. Make up descants for songs.

Sing the "Tallis Canon" as a one-part song, then as a round. See if other one-part songs can be made into rounds.

Other Activities

Compare religious music and religious paintings:

LAST SUPPER painted by Leonardo da Vinci in 1494.

SISTINE MADONNA painted by Raphael.

"The Messiah" composed by Handel.

"Ave Maria" composed by Victoria, Bach-Gounod, or Schubert.

Build a picture unit on the development of the organ and of the bells.

Study the evolution of musical notation and place the findings in notebooks.

Study the various forms of sacred choral music such as:

Motet	Cantata	Mass
Chorale	Oratorio	Hymn

Study the lives of composers of sacred choral music:

Luther	Bach	Handel
Palestrina	Praetorius	Mozart

Study the development of vocal music:

Plain song (one voice)

Antiphonal (two choir responsive style)

Organum and descant

Polyphonic style (many voices)

Music Reading Assignments

Lomax, John A. and Alan. AMERICAN BALLADS AND FOLK SONGS. The Macmillan Company, New York, 1934.

Negro Spirituals   Page 580
White Spirituals   Page 563

Carter, Phyllis Anne. THE BANDS PLAY ON. Robert M. McBride
and Company, New York, 1942.

Royalty and the Church   Page 82

Johnson, James Weldon. BOOK OF AMERICAN NEGRO SPIRITUALS.
The Viking Press, New York, 1925.

Spiritual Music   Page 11

Bigelow, Arthur Lynds. CARILLON. Princeton University Press,
Princeton, New Jersey, 1948.

McKinney, Anderson. DISCOVERING MUSIC. American Book
Company, Chicago, 1934.

Golden Age, A   Page 212
Illustrations of 16th Century Choir   Page 215
King of Instruments, The   Chapter XXXV
Pre-Bach   Chapter XXVII
Summary of Historical Developments   Page 221

Rayner, Edwin. FAMOUS CATHEDRALS. Grosset and Dunlap, Incorporated, New York, 1936.

Rayner, Edwin. FAMOUS STATUES AND THEIR STORIES. Grosset
and Dunlap, Incorporated, New York, 1936.

Schwimmer, Franciska. GREAT MUSICIANS AS CHILDREN. Doubleday, Doran and Company, Garden City, New York, 1929.

Johann Sebastian Bach   Page 105

Buchanan, Fannie L. HOW MAN MADE MUSIC. Wilcox and Follet
Company, Chicago, 1941.

Forms of Church Music
  Beginning in 1600   Page 145

Bauer, Peyser. HOW MUSIC GREW. G. P. Putnam's Sons, New
York, 1925.

Bach, The Giant   Chapter XVIII

Music in Merrie England   Chapter XIV
Organs, Organists, and Organ Works Chapter XVII
Reformation   Chapter XII
What Church Music Imported   Chapter VII
 from Greece

Bernstein, Martin. INTRODUCTION TO MUSIC. Prentice-Hall, Incorporated, New York, 1937.

Bach's Organ Music   Pages 78, 87
Church Cantatas   Page 87
Johann Sebastian Bach   Page 57
Mass in B Minor   Page 93
Passion Music   Page 90
Polyphony and Harmony   Chapter IV

Jones, Barnard. INTRODUCTION TO MUSICAL KNOWLEDGE. Paul A. Schmitt Music Company, Minneapolis, Minnesota, 1935.

Bach   Pages 55, 102, 121
Church Music   Pages 37, 44
Early Instruments—The Organ Page 49
Form   Page 63
Handel   Pages 103, 126
Haydn   Pages 56, 103, 128
Luther   Page 44
Palestrina   Page 45

KEYBOARD JUNIOR. 1346 Chapel Street, New Haven 11, Connecticut.

George Frederick Handel
    Volume IV, No. 3, December, 1950 Page 2
Messiah, The
    Volume IV, No. 3, December, 1950 Page 4
Organ, The
    Volume IV, No. 3, December, 1950 Page 6
Rachmaninoff—Interpreter of Russia's Bells
    Volume V, No. 1, October, 1946 Page 1
Song of the Bells
    Volume IV, No. 3, December, 1950 Page 7

Baldwin, Lillian. A LISTENER'S ANTHOLOGY OF MUSIC, VOLUME 1. Silver Burdett Company, Chicago, 1948.

Artist, The	Page 47
Messiah, The	Page 50
Mr. Handel of London	Chapter II
"Xerxes" — Largo	Page 56

Stringham, Edwin John. LISTENING TO MUSIC CREATIVELY. Prentice-Hall, Incorporated, New York, 1946.

Music and Religion	Page 17

Gee, Leeder, Wilson. LOG FOR MUSIC AMERICANS SING. Silver Burdett Company, New York, 1949.

Hymn Tunes	Page 4

Hartshorn, Leavitt. THE MENTOR (Making Friends with Music). Ginn and Company, Chicago, 1940.

Pastoral Symphony from "The Messiah"	Page 241

Kinscella, Hazel G. MUSIC AND ROMANCE. RCA Victor Company, Camden, New Jersey, 1930.

Music of the Church: Motet, Chorale, Cantata, and Oratorio	Page 424
Pipe Organ and Its Music, The	Page 504

McKinney, Anderson. MUSIC IN HISTORY. American Book Company, Chicago, 1940.

Development of the Plain Song	Page 122
Early Hymns	Page 126

Siegmeister, Elie (Edited by). MUSIC LOVER'S HANDBOOK. William Morrow and Company, New York, 1943.

George Frederick Handel	Page 347
Oratorio, Cantata, and Mass, The	Page 132

Bauer, Peyser. MUSIC THROUGH THE AGES. G. P. Putnam's Sons, New York, 1932.

Keyboard Instruments	Chapter XIV

UNIT V (Grade VII)

Music and Transportation

Locomotion to Music

Oars dipping rhythmically, train wheels moving steadily, an airplane soaring smoothly into the sky all lend themselves to songs and rhythmic movement.

Singing

McConathy et al. AMERICAN MUSIC HORIZONS. Silver Burdett Company, Chicago, 1951.

Pat Works on the Railway American Work Song Page 69

Bridgman, Curtis. THE AMERICAN SINGER, BOOK VII. American Book Company, Chicago, 1947.

Camptown Races, The Foster Page 143

Bridgman, Curtis. THE AMERICAN SINGER, BOOK VIII. American Book Company, Chicago, 1948.

Dip, Paddle, Dip	Valentine	Page 37
In the Boat	Grieg	Page 71
Song My Paddle Sings	Bridgman	Page 59

Dykema, Pitcher, Vandevere. LET MUSIC RING! C. C. Birchard and Company, Boston, 1947.

Captain of the Pinafore, The	Sullivan	Page 132
In My Wagon	Dutch Folk Song	Page 81
Life on the Ocean Wave, A	Old American Song	Page 44
Skye Boat Song	Scottish Folk Song	Page 69
Yankee Ship and a Yankee Crew, A	Early American	Page 129

McConathy, Beattie, Morgan. MUSIC OF MANY LANDS AND PEO-
PLES. Silver Burdett Company, Chicago, 1932.

A Boat! A Boat!	Old English Round	Page 120
As I Put Off from Shore	Italian	Page 218

Dykema, Pitcher, Stevens, Vandevere. SING OUT! C. C. Birchard
and Company, Boston, 1946.

I've Been Working on the Railroad	American	Page 152
John Paul Jones	Netherland	Page 87
New River Train	Early American Song	Page 48
Prayer for All Airmen, A	Peters	Page 235
Sailing Song	Gibney	Page 156
Wait for the Wagon	Buckley	Page 49
We Sing of Sails	Coerne	Page 241

Glenn, Leavitt, Rebmann. SONG PARADE. Ginn and Company,
Chicago, 1941.

Coachman, The	Russian Folk Song	Page 140
Sailing	Marks	Page 167

Glenn, Leavitt, Rebmann, Baker. TREASURE. Ginn and Company, Chicago, 1938.

Westward Ho!	Strickland	Page 106

Rhythm Activities

Most of the songs may be interpreted with rhythm movements.
Instruments such as triangles for oars, maracas for trains, shakers for planes, etc. may be used effectively.

Learn the dance for *A Life on the Ocean Wave* on page 44 in
LET MUSIC RING! Make up dances for other transportation songs.

Audio-Visual Aids

1. Recordings

Boating on the Lake (Kullak)	RCA Rhythm II
In the Boat (Grieg)	RCA Singing IV

Little Train of the Caipira (Villa - Lobos)

Old Man River, from "Show Boat" (Kern)

On the Trail, from "Grand Canyon Suite" (Grofé)

Pacific 231 (Honegger)

Pat Works on the Railway (American Folk Song)

Regiment Was Riding, The, sung by the Don Cossacks, Jaroff, Director

Sleigh Ride (Mozart)

Surrey with the Fringe on Top, from "Oklahoma!" (Rodgers)

Tramp, Tramp, Tramp Along the Highway, from "Naughty Marietta" (Herbert)

Volga Boatmen, The (Russian Folk Tune)

2. Films

ANY WAY TO GET THERE.   Teaching Film Custodians, Inc.

Unusual means of transportation throughout the world include donkeys in Greece, burros in Jerusalem, and camels in Egypt.

CANADIAN PACIFIC.   Films Incorporated.

This film tells the story of the men who pushed the Canadian Pacific Railroad through the wilderness of the Canadian Rockies. Man and nature combined in an attempt to halt this western movement to no avail.

DEVELOPMENT OF   Encyclopaedia Britannica
TRANSPORTATION.   Films, Inc.

The dramatic story of the development of transportation in the United States is traced in this film. It calls attention to the natural barriers which compelled isolation and slowed up expansion when the nation was young, and it points out the developments which broke down these barriers.

PACIFIC 231.   MENC Handbook.

A skillful interpretation of a modern symphonic poem about a railroad locomotive is shown. Exciting visual images of a powerful engine in operation as well as its run are remarkably well synchronized with the spirit and character of Honegger's music.

TRAFFIC.	Teaching Film Custodians, Inc.

This study of types of transportation in many countries also affords glimpses of national costumes.

Supplementary Films:

AIRPLANE TRIP.	Encyclopaedia Britannica Films, Inc.
ARTERIES OF NEW YORK.	Encyclopaedia Britannica Films, Inc.
GOLDEN JOURNEY.	Ideal Pictures.
LITTLE OLD NEW YORK.	Films Incorporated.
NORTHWARD TO NOME.	Ideal Pictures.
PIONEERS OF THE PLAINS.	Encyclopaedia Britannica Films, Inc.
'ROUND SOUTH AMERICA BY AIR.	Ideal Pictures.
TRANSPORTATION IN THE U.S.A.	The March of Time Forum Films.
WHEELS OF PROGRESS.	Ideal Pictures.
WINGS TO ENGLAND AND BELGIUM.	Ideal Pictures.
WINGS TO HAWAII.	Ideal Pictures.

Creative Activities

Since so many of the transportation songs are about boats and other sailing craft, the students may enjoy making up tunes about various kinds of boats such as canoes, rowboats, ocean liners, and sailboats.

Through song, the history and development of transportation can be studied.

A simple operetta or pageant might be worked out beginning with the earliest forms of locomotion.

Other Activities

Find illustrations for all modes of transportation and place them in the notebooks. Favorite songs to go with each type of transportation might also be included.

Study the life of the inventor of the steam engine and of the airplane. Aviators such as Charles Lindbergh, Eddie Rickenbacker, "home-town" flyers, etc. will be interesting to study.

The Dance as Used in Music

Natural Folk Expression, the Source of Our Dance

Folk dances of many kinds and from many countries, dances of the Indian and Negro, square and circle dances serve as a basis for interesting study.

Singing

McConathy et al. AMERICAN MUSIC HORIZONS. Silver Burdett Company, Chicago, 1951.

Kerry Dance	Malloy	Page 235

Bridgman, Curtis. THE AMERICAN SINGER BOOK VII. American Book Company, Chicago, 1947.

Old Time Dance, An	Curtis	Page 155

Dykema, Pitcher, Vandevere. LET MUSIC RING! C. C. Birchard and Company, Boston, 1949.

Barn Dance	American Tune	Page 42
Csardas	Hungarian Folk Dance	Page 80
Dancing Together	Polish Folk Tune	Page 79
Nelly Bly	Foster	Page 46
Square Dance	Perry	Page 39

Wilson, Leeder, Gee. MUSIC AMERICANS SING. Silver Burdett Company, Chicago, 1948.

Mooje Moccasin	Ojibway Indians (Minnesota)	Page 20
Oh, Susanna!	Foster	Page 59
Rosa-becka-lina	American Mountain Song	Page 89

McConathy, Beattie, Morgan. MUSIC HIGHWAYS AND BYWAYS. Silver Burdett Company, Chicago, 1936.

Wilson, Leeder, Gee, Greer. MUSIC THE WORLD SINGS. Silver Burdett Company, Chicago, 1952.

Dykema, Pitcher, Stevens, Vandevere. SING OUT! C. C. Birchard and Company, Boston, 1946.

McConathy et al. WORLD MUSIC HORIZONS. Silver Burdett Company, Chicago, 1951.

Rhythm Activities

Dance directions will be found with many of the songs listed above. Work those out as suggested or make adaptations to fit the needs of the group.

Encourage the boys and girls to learn to call square dances. Within a class a callers' group could be organized. If there is a square dance club in the community, they might be invited to put on a demonstration for the students. Also, if there are experienced callers in the community, invite them to talk with the class and give suggestions and demonstrations.

When the common circle and square dances and the Virginia Reel have been mastered, adapt these steps and formations to other music.

Teach the waltz, the minuet, and others of the classic dances to the students. The schottische and the polka should also become a part of their repertoire.

The following books have many fine suggestions for dances:

HANDY COUNTRY DANCE BOOK.

> Cooperative Recreation Service, Delaware, Ohio.

HANDY PLAY PARTY BOOK.

> Cooperative Recreation Service, Delaware, Ohio.

QUADRILLES.

> Cooperative Recreation Service, Delaware, Ohio.

On the following pages in AMERICAN MUSIC HORIZONS directions are found for a number of dances: Pages 58, 91, 101, 138, 143, 208, and 278. Even though all of the dances are not learned, the students will find them interesting to look through. Additional dance directions are found in WORLD MUSIC HORIZONS on pages 64, 103, and 139.

Audio-Visual Aids

1. Recordings

   Amaryllis (Ghys)   RCA Album IV—Rhythm

   Anitra's Dance, from "Peer Gynt Suite" (Grieg), played by the London Philharmonic—Goosens, conductor

   Arabian Dance, from the "Nutcracker Suite" (Tschaikowsky), played by the New York Philharmonic—Rodzinsky, conductor

   Ballet (Gluck)   RCA Album I—Rhythm

   Blue Danube (Strauss)

   Bolero (Ravel)

   Country Dances (Mozart)   RCA Album VI—Rhythm

   Country Gardens (Grainger)

Dance Chinois, from the "Nutcracker Suite" (Tschaikow-sky)

Emperor Waltz (Strauss)

Firebird Suite (Stravinsky)

Folk Dance (Beethoven)

Gavottes (Bach)

Hungarian Dance No. 2 in D Minor (Brahms)

Hungarian Dances (Brahms)   RCA Album VI—Listening

Minuet, from "Don Juan"

  (Mozart)   RCA Album V—Rhythm

Rhapsodie Espagnole (Ravel)

Square Dances, performed by Woodhull's Masters

Turkey in the Straw (arranged by Guion)

Further suggestions for listening might include recordings of dance forms such as: allemande, bolero, bourree, czardas, gigue, habanera, hornpipe, mazurka, polka, polonaise, reel, sarabande, tango, and tarantella. Analyze each for meter and swing. Popular dance tunes should be analyzed for meter and swing, also. Interesting discussions may be had concerning the modern dance orchestras and their leaders.

2. Films

BEAUTIFUL BLUE DANUBE WALTZ.   MENC Handbook.

The Vienna Symphony Orchestra conducted by Robert Stolz plays this popular waltz by Johann Strauss. Dancing is done by members of the Vienna Statts - Opera Ballet.

OPTICAL POEM, AN.   MENC Handbook.

An orchestral performance of Liszt's "Second Hungarian Rhapsody" is synchronized with moving geometric figures in color.

PEOPLE DANCE, THE.   MENC Handbook.

Dancing related to various social and economic backgrounds is shown. Pioneer square dances, quadrilles, and modern jive are shown, as well as Indian religious dances.

Supplementary Films:

BALLET DE SANTONS.	MENC Handbook.
CEREMONIAL DANCES.	MENC Handbook.
DANCES OF THE NATIONS.	Bell and Howell Company.
DANCING FLEECES, THE.	British Information Services.
FABLE OF THE PEACOCK, THE.	MENC Handbook.
GREAT WALTZ, THE.	MENC Handbook.
MARY VISITS POLAND.	MENC Handbook.
MOOR'S PAVANE, THE.	MENC Handbook.
NATIVE AFRICA.	MENC Handbook.
NORWEGIAN FOLK DANCES.	MENC Handbook.
OLD VIENNA, HOME OF WALTZES.	Ideal Pictures Corporation.
RHYTHM OF AFRICA.	MENC Handbook.
RUSSIAN BALLET AND FOLK DANCES.	MENC Handbook.
SHE AND MOON DANCE.	MENC Handbook.
SIBELIUS (SCARAMOUCHE BALLET EXCERPTS).	MENC Handbook.
SPANISH GYPSIES.	MENC Handbook.
STEPS OF THE BALLET.	MENC Handbook.
SWAN LAKE BALLET.	MENC Handbook.
TWO CHINESE DANCES.	MENC Handbook.
WALTZ IN A FLAT MAJOR.	MENC Handbook.
WORLD DANCES, THE.	Ideal Pictures Corporation.

Creative Activities

Make up as many dances as possible. A very natural outgrowth of this unit might be a folk dance festival — a "Dance of All Nations" type of production. If this is done, have the students design and make their own costumes. Suggest that the students make rhythm instruments to accompany the dancing.

Other Activities

A mural might be made depicting a variety of dances.

Study the ballet; become familiar with ballet terms and names of ballet dancers and ballet troupes.

Study the life of Martha Graham and other contemporary dancers.

Included in notebooks might be a history of the dance since its beginning.

Music Reading Assignments

Surette, Mason. APPRECIATION OF MUSIC. The Baker and Taylor Company, New York, 1910.
Dance and Its Development, The   Page 48

Wheeler, Opal. SEBASTIAN BACH — THE BOY FROM THURINGIA. E. P. Dutton and Company, Incorporated, New York, 1937.

Society for Curriculum Study Incorporated. BUILDING AMERICA VOLUME VII, NO. 8 (Periodical). New York, 1942.

Goss, Madeleine. DEEP FLOWING BROOK. Henry Holt and Company, New York, 1938.

Ford, Mr. and Mrs. Henry. GOOD MORNING. Dearborn, Michigan, 1943.
Music Calls and Directions for Old Time Dancing

Bauer, Peyser. HOW MUSIC GREW. G. P. Putnam's Sons, New York, 1925.

Bach, The Giant	Chapter XVIII
Dance Tunes Grow Up — Suites	Chapter XV
Dancing of Primitive Man	Pages 4, 6
Influence of Negro Dances on	
American Music	Page 143

National Portraits in Folk Music	Chapter X
Origin of the Suite	Page 126
People Dance and Sing, The	Chapter IX

Bernstein, Martin. INTRODUCTION TO MUSIC. Prentice-Hall, Incorporated, New York, 1937.

Orchestral Suite in D	Page 81

Jones, Barnard. INTRODUCTION TO MUSICAL KNOWLEDGE. Paul A. Schmitt Music Company, Minneapolis, Minnesota, 1935.

Dance Forms	Page 75

Kinscella, Hazel G. KINSCELLA READER, BOOK IV. The University Publishing Company, 1926.

Johann Strauss, the Waltz King	Page 129

Baldwin, Lillian. A LISTENER'S ANTHOLOGY OF MUSIC, VOLUME I. Silver Burdett Company, Chicago, 1948.

Artists, The	Page 224
Brahms, a Musical Philosopher	Chapter VII
Hungarian Dances No. 5 and 6	Page 237

Baldwin, Lillian. A LISTENER'S ANTHOLOGY OF MUSIC, VOLUME II. Silver Burdett Company, Chicago, 1948.

Artist, The	Page 113
Edvard Hagerup Grieg	Page 105
Firebird Suite, The (Ballet Suite)	Page 411
Igor Stravinsky	Page 408
Mazurka in B Flat Minor, Opus 7, No. 1	Page 83
Music and the Ballet	Page 397
Peer Gynt Suite No. 1	Page 117
Polonaise in A Major, Opus 40	Page 81
Valse in C Sharp Minor, Opus 64, No. 2	Page 85

Kinscella, Hazel G. MUSIC AND ROMANCE. RCA Victor Company, Camden, New Jersey, 1930.

Ballet	Pages 154, 162, 174, 396
Classic Suite	Page 102
Folk Music of the New World	Page 48
Folk Music of the Old World	Page 24
Music in This Century	Page 205
Suites: Contrast in Dances—	
Serial Story-Telling	Page 157

McKinney, Anderson. MUSIC IN HISTORY. American Book Company, Chicago, 1940.

Dance Songs of the Time	Page 187
Dancing: Primitive, Egyptian, Minoan, Greek, Roman, Early Christian, Middle Ages, Sixteenth and Seventeenth Century Waltz	

Siegmeister, Elie (Edited by). MUSIC LOVER'S HANDBOOK. William Morrow and Company, New York, 1943.

Ballet and Music	Page 298

Kinscella, Hazel G. MUSIC ON THE AIR. The Viking Press, New York, 1934.

Folk Dance and the Ballet	Page 89

Bauer, Peyser. MUSIC THROUGH THE AGES. G. P. Putnam's Sons, New York, 1932.

Folk Music Through the Ages	Chapter X

Hartshorn, Leavitt. THE PILOT. (Making Friends with Music). Ginn and Company, Chicago, 1940.

Blue Danube Waltz	Page 83
Nutcracker Suite	Page 39

Hartshorn, Leavitt. PRELUDE. (Making Friends with Music.) Ginn and Company, Chicago, 1940.

Ballet Music from "Faust"	Page 29
Blue Danube Waltz	Page 113
Nutcracker Suite	Page 41

UNIT VII (Grade VIII)

Music from Our Latin-American Neighbors

Intercultural Relations through Music

The enchanting melodies and rhythms of our neighbors to the south open new doors to a greater understanding of Latin-American people and their cultures.

Singing

Glenn, Leavitt, Rebmann, Baker. ADVENTURE. Ginn and Company, Chicago, 1938.

On the Brow of the Hill	Mexican	Page 156
Ship of Rio, The	South American	Page 158

Leavitt, Kilduff, Freeman. ADVENTURES IN SINGING. C. C. Birchard and Company, Boston, 1952.

El Charro	Latin-American	Page 99
Gay Caballero, The	Mexican	Page 10
Pepita	Mexican	Page 119

McConathy et al. AMERICAN MUSIC HORIZONS. Silver Burdett Company, Chicago, 1952.

Charcoal Man	Mexican	Page 254
Cucaracha, La	Mexican	Page 260

Bridgman, Curtis. AMERICAN SINGER BOOK VIII. American Book Company, Chicago, 1948.

Afternoon in May, An	Latin-American Folk Song	Page 76
I'm Far from Homeland	Mexican Folk Song	Page 82
Magic Boat, The	Brazilian Folk Song	Page 66
Morning Serenade	Mexican Folk Song	Page 96

Dykema, Pitcher, Vandevere. LET MUSIC RING! C. C. Birchard and Company, Boston, 1949.

| *Beautiful Eyes, The* | Brazilian | Page 67 |

McConathy, Beattie, Morgan. MUSIC HIGHWAYS AND BYWAYS. Silver Burdett Company, Chicago, 1936.

Adios Te Digo	Argentine Folk Song	Page 107
Buy My Tortillas	Chilean Folk Song	Page 110
Flower of Changunga	Mexican	Page 114
My Pretty Cabocla	Brazilian	Page 105
Palapala	Argentine Folk Song	Page 108
Yaravi	Peruvian Folk Song	Page 113

Dykema, Pitcher, Stevens, Vandevere. SING OUT! C. C. Birchard and Company, Boston, 1946.

| *Chiapanecas* | Mexican | Page 64 |

Note: Many fine songs are to be found in THE LATIN-AMERICAN SONG BOOK, Ginn and Company, 1942 and AMIGOS, Cooperative Recreation Service, Delaware, Ohio.

Rhythm Activities

Have as many Latin-American rhythm instruments available as possible: maracas, castanets, tambourines, bonga and conga drums, guiros, xylophones, marimbas, etc. If desired, many of these instruments can be made by the children in school.* Unless there is a shop or workroom near the music room, however, it might be a better idea to have the instruments made at home. Use these instruments freely with the songs and phonograph recordings. Do much clapping of rhythm patterns.

Have a demonstration of the tango, rhumba, samba. If there are no junior high students who have learned these dances, bring in adults who can do them. In some communities there

---

* Thompson and Nordholm, KEYS TO TEACHING ELEMENTARY SCHOOL MUSIC. Paul A. Schmitt Music Company, Minneapolis, Minnesota, 1949. Pages 67-68. Coleman, CREATIVE MUSIC FOR CHILDREN. Pages 136-137.
McLaughlin and Stanchfield, CANCIONCITAS. Paul A. Schmitt Music Company, Minneapolis, Minnesota, 1948.

are professional dancers who would be happy to give a demonstration to the group.

Teach the conga.

Directions: Form a line. The step is one, two, three, kick out to the side, one, two, three, kick, etc. Place hands on waist of person in front; weave in and out snake-fashion. Start slowly; increase the speed as skill develops.

Audio-Visual Aids

1. Recordings

Bachianas Brasileiras No. 5 (Villa-Lobos)
Corcovado (Milhaud)
El Salon Mexico (Copland)
Espana Rapsodie (Chabrier)
Native Brazilian Music
Song of the Black Swan (Villa-Lobos)
Tango (Poldowsky)

Argentine—*Vidalita*	RCA Album V—Singing
Brazil—*Tutu Maramba*	RCA Album V—Singing
Chile—*Flowing River*	RCA Album V—Singing
Cuba—*Cuba*	RCA Album V—Singing
Ecuador—*Santo San Juanito*	RCA Album V—Singing
Mexican—*Que Lejos Estoy*	RCA Album V—Singing
Mexican—*Uy! Tara LaLa*	RCA Album V—Singing
Peru—*From Yon Mountain Verdant*	RCA Album V—Singing
Puerto Rico—*To Bethlehem, Singing*	RCA Album V—Singing

Further suggestions for listening:

Other folk songs. Authentic recordings are available from the Library of Congress.

Primitive folk music of the isolated Indians in the hinterlands of Mexico.

Songs connected with the religious rites of the natives.

2. Films

FIESTAS OF THE HILLS.   MENC Handbook.

Symbolic dances and elaborate processionals are shown as part of a religious fiesta in Mexico.

FIRE AND WATER.   MENC Handbook.

Scenes on Candlemas Day are filmed in the beautiful city of Taxco during Passion Week. Native religious dances and music accompany the ritual of villagers bringing symbols of their daily lives to the cathedral to be blessed.

PEOPLE OF MEXICO.   MENC Handbook.

Folk music and dances of the working people as well as arts and occupations are interestingly shown.

Supplementary Films:

AI-YE (Mankind).	MENC Handbook.
FILMS OF THE LATIN-AMERICAN COUNTRIES AND THE PACIFIC ISLANDS.	U.S. Government Films.
ITURBI, JOSE (Reel 1)	MENC Handbook.
LATIN RHYTHMS WITH JAN PIERCE AND LUBA MALINA.	Eastin Pictures, Inc.
MEXICAN MOODS.	MENC Handbook.
RHYTHM FROM CUBA.	Ideal Pictures Corp.
SPANISH GYPSIES.	MENC Handbook.
SUNDAY MORNING IN MEXICO.	MENC Handbook.

3. Other Visual Aids

Make map of Latin-America.

Study the paintings and architecture of the Latin-American small countries.

· Creative Activities

Besides making instruments create Latin-American rhythm patterns.

Write songs.

Write harmony parts to one-part songs.

Other Activities

Have pupils draw a music map of Latin-America showing, in the proper places on the map, something of the characteristics of the different songs and dances.

Check the students' vocabularies of words and terms peculiar to Latin-American music.

Notebooks:

Insert appropriate pictures—original or clipped from magazines.
Enumerate characteristic rhythm patterns.
Include notes from class reports on composers and performers.

Music Reading Assignments

Ewen, David. THE BOOK OF MODERN COMPOSERS. Alfred A. Knopf, New York, 1947.

Carlos Chavez	Pages 19, 433
Heitor Villa-Lobos	Page 14
Julian Carillo	Page 421

Rothery, Agnes. CENTRAL AMERICAN ROUND-ABOUTS. Dodd, Mead and Company, Incorporated, San Francisco, California, 1947.

Dances, Holidays, and Pilgrimages   Page 33

Hanson, Earl Parker. CHILE—THE LAND OF PROGRESS. Reynal and Hitchcock, New York, 1947.

Culture   Chapter IV

KEYBOARD JUNIOR. 1346 Chapel Street, New Haven 11, Connecticut.

Maurice Ravel—The Composer of the Famous Bolero
Volume III, No. 8, May, 1945.   Page 6.

Volume V, No. 5, February, 1947. (entire issue)
Volume X, No. 6, March, 1952. (entire issue)

Goetz, Delia. LET'S READ ABOUT SOUTH AMERICA. The Fideler
Company, Grand Rapids, Michigan, 1950.

South American Art	Chapter XIII

LIFE MAGAZINE. Time Incorporated, 540 N. Michigan Avenue,
Chicago, Illinois, October 6, 1947.

Cuba's Number One Composer,	
Ernesto Lecuona	Page 145
Cuba's Tin-Pan Alley	Page 145

Baldwin, Lillian. A LISTENER'S ANTHOLOGY OF MUSIC, VOLUME II.
Silver Burdett Company, Chicago, 1948.

Latin Americana	Page 522

McKinney, Howard D. MUSIC AND MAN. American Book Company, Chicago, 1948.

Popular Music in the Americas	
South of Us	Page 125

Kinscella, Hazel G. MUSIC AND ROMANCE. RCA Victor Company,
Camden, New Jersey, 1930.

Pan American Music	Page 265

Stokowski, Leopold. MUSIC FOR ALL. Simon Schuster, New York,
1943.

Latin-American Instruments

Siegmeister, Elie (Edited by). MUSIC LOVER'S HANDBOOK. William Morrow and Company, New York, 1943.

Mexican Popular Music	Page 29

Goetz, Delia. NEIGHBORS TO THE SOUTH. Harcourt, Brace and
Company, New York, 1944.

NEW YORK TIMES. New York Times Company, New York.

Serious Composers of Cuba	April 29, 1945

Brown, Bailey. OUR LATIN-AMERICAN NEIGHBORS. Houghton Mifflin Company, New York, 1944.

Music in Brazil	Page 424
Music in Mexico	Pages 175, 456
Music Is Part of Life to Latin-Americans	Page 456

Peck, Anne Merriman. PAGEANT OF SOUTH AMERICAN HISTORY. Longman's Green and Company, New York, 1941.

Bells, Drums, Flutes, Whistles	Page 16
Church Music	Pages 119, 212
Don Joao and Music	Page 306
Flutes, Bells, Pan Pipes, and Trumpets	Page 57
Flutes, Drums, Gourd Rattles	Page 6
Indian Music—Music in South America Now	Page 378
Music in Colonial Time	Pages 156, 176, 198
Spanish, Portuguese, Negro, and Indian Influences	Page 372

UNIT VIII (Grade VIII)

Evolution of Jazz
An Aspect of Our American Music

What is jazz? How did it begin? Does it have any musical merit? Is it a part of our American heritage? Is it characteristic of our way of life?

Singing

Glenn, Leavitt, Rebmann, Baker. ADVENTURE. Ginn and Company, Chicago, 1938.

Goin' to Shout All over		
God's Heaven	Spiritual	Page 65
Inchin' Along	Negro Spiritual	Page 54

Leavitt, Kilduff, Freeman. ADVENTURES IN SINGING. C. C. Birchard and Company, Boston, 1952.

Don't Grow Weary Traveler	Negro Spiritual	Page 72
Don't Min' What Satan Say	Spiritual	Page 78
Early in the Mornin'	Spiritual	Page 68
I Believe I Will Go		
Back Home	Spiritual	Page 74
I Can't Stay Away	Negro Spiritual	Page 76

McConathy et al. AMERICAN MUSIC HORIZONS. Silver Burdett Company, Chicago, 1951.

Battle of Jericho	Spiritual	Page 76
Oh, A-Rock-a-My Soul	Spiritual	Page 66

Bridgman, Curtis. THE AMERICAN SINGER BOOK VIII. American Book Company, Chicago, 1948.

Go Down Moses	Negro Spiritual	Page 144
Little Wheel A-Turnin'	Spiritual	Page 13

A minstrel show could be a natural outgrowth of this unit and dances could be created, costumes designed, an original script with an interlocutor written, etc.

Other Activities

Study the lives of famous Negro personalities such as James Bland, Marian Anderson, Dorothy Maynor, Katherine Dunham, Nathaniel Dett, and Roland Hayes.

Study the lives of other great Negroes such as George Washington Carver, Booker T. Washington, James Weldon Johnson, Jesse Owens, and Dr. Charles Drew.

Study the styles of jazz band leaders.

Insert appropriate pictures and favorite rhythm patterns in notebooks. Include a tracing of the history of the development of jazz.

Music Reading Assignments

Lomax, John A. and Alan. AMERICAN BALLADS AND FOLK SONGS. The Macmillan Company, New York, 1934.

Creole, Mountain, White Minstrel, etc.	Pages 211-299
Spirituals	Pages 577-610

Van Loon, Hendrik Willem. THE ARTS. Simon and Schuster, New York, 1937.

Chopin, The Originator of the Modern Nationalistic "Blues"	Page 609

Hartshorn, Leavitt. AT HOME AND ABROAD. (Making Friends with Music). Ginn and Company, Chicago, 1940.

Bess, You Is My Woman Now	Page 42
Rhapsody in Blue	Page 39

Carter, Phyllis Anne. THE BANDS PLAY ON. Robert M. Mcbride and Company, New York, 1942.

Today's Bands and Orchestras	Chapter XI

McConathy et al. WORLD MUSIC HORIZONS. Silver Burdett Company, Chicago, 1951.

Climbin' Up the Mountain   Negro Spiritual   Page 104

The students will want to sing current hit tunes. Along with this unit some of that is acceptable—even desirable; however, use discretion and some restrictions as to what is to be sung. Many texts are not suitable for teen-agers. Encourage the singing of such melodies as "The Syncopated Clock", "Swinging on a Star", "Oh, What a Beautiful Morning", etc.

Rhythm Activities

Use bones, rattles, and shakers for rhythm accompaniment to songs. Spoons and pieces of wood or the traditional bones (spare-rib bones used in minstrel shows) may be used.

Clap the regular pulse of the music, clap the off-beat, then clap the syncopated rhythm. Divide the class in two groups: one group claps the regular pulse, the other group claps the off-beat.

Request a member of the class who is studying dancing to give a demonstration of "soft shoe", "buck and wing", "hoedown", etc. The class will enjoy learning some of these steps.

From the "toe-heel shuffle" a simple jitter-bug may be done.

Audio-Visual Aids

1. Recordings
   Dere's No Hiding Place Down Dere (Spiritual)
   Every Time I Feel de Spirit (Spiritual)
   From the Canebrake (Dett)
   Grand Canyon Suite (Grofé)
   Here de Lambs A-Crying (Spiritual)
   Ol' Man River from "Showboat" (Kern)
   Porgy and Bess (Gershwin)
   Rhapsody in Blue (Gershwin)
   Water Boy
   Were You There? (Spiritual)

Dykema, Pitcher, Vandevere. LET MUSIC RING! C. C. Birchard and Company, Boston, 1949.

Cotton Needs Pickin'	Negro Work Song	Page 25
Old Ship of Zion, The	White Spiritual	Page 103
Roll, Jordan, Roll	Negro Spiritual	Page 98
Sinner, Please Don't Let This Harvest Pass	Spiritual	Page 100
Somebody's Knocking at Your Door	Negro Spiritual	Page 98
When the Love Comes Trick-a-lin' Down	Negro Spiritual	Page 99

Wilson, Leeder, Gee. MUSIC AMERICANS SING. Silver Burdett Company, Chicago, 1948.

A-Rockin' All Night	Negro Spiritual	Page 117
De Creation	West Virginia	Page 60
Dese Bones	Negro Song	Page 50
Go Tell It on the Mountain	Negro Spiritual	Page 125
Little David Play on Your Harp	Negro Spiritual	Page 71
Long Distance Blues	Negro Blues Song	Page 70
Nobody Knows the Trouble I've Seen	Spiritual	Page 63
Poor Wayfaring Stranger	White Spiritual	Page 76
Rise Up Shepherd and Follow	Negro Spiritual	Page 126
Rock O' Jubilee	Negro Jubilee	Page 73
Shortnin' Bread	Negro Song	Page 69
Sign of de Judgment	Negro Spiritual	Page 72
Swing Low, Sweet Chariot	Negro Spiritual	Page 62

Wilson, Leeder, Gee, Greer. MUSIC THE WORLD SINGS. Silver Burdett Company, Chicago, 1952.

Dry Bones	Negro Spiritual	Page 46
Swing Time in School Time	Fields	Page 125

McConathy et al. WORLD MUSIC HORIZONS. Silver Burdett Company, Chicago, 1951.

Climbin' Up the Mountain   Negro Spiritual   Page 104

The students will want to sing current hit tunes. Along with this unit some of that is acceptable—even desirable; however, use discretion and some restrictions as to what is to be sung. Many texts are not suitable for teen-agers. Encourage the singing of such melodies as "The Syncopated Clock", "Swinging on a Star", "Oh, What a Beautiful Morning", etc.

Rhythm Activities

Use bones, rattles, and shakers for rhythm accompaniment to songs. Spoons and pieces of wood or the traditional bones (spare-rib bones used in minstrel shows) may be used.

Clap the regular pulse of the music, clap the off-beat, then clap the syncopated rhythm. Divide the class in two groups: one group claps the regular pulse, the other group claps the off-beat.

Request a member of the class who is studying dancing to give a demonstration of "soft shoe", "buck and wing", "hoe-down", etc. The class will enjoy learning some of these steps.

From the "toe-heel shuffle" a simple jitter-bug may be done.

Audio-Visual Aids

1. Recordings
   Dere's No Hiding Place Down Dere (Spiritual)
   Every Time I Feel de Spirit (Spiritual)
   From the Canebrake (Dett)
   Grand Canyon Suite (Grofé)
   Here de Lambs A-Crying (Spiritual)
   Ol' Man River from "Showboat" (Kern)
   Porgy and Bess (Gershwin)
   Rhapsody in Blue (Gershwin)
   Water Boy
   Were You There? (Spiritual)

Pupils will be eager to bring records. From these, suitable selections may be played for the class. Again, as in singing, use discretion as to the type of music to be played for the class.

2. Films

ALEXANDER'S RAGTIME BAND.   Films Incorporated.

This is the story of the first recognition of jazz as a truly American art form using Irving Berlin's music against a background of the Barbary Coast of San Francisco.

BE GONE DULL CARE.   MENC Handbook

The Oscar Peterson Trio plays jazz music that is interpreted in restless lines, colors, and forms that change with the rhythm of the music.

BUBBLING OVER

(Ethel Waters).   Ideal Pictures Corp.

LIFE IN OLD LOUISIANA.   MENC Handbook

The Delta country of the Mississippi River is shown— customs, manners, music, architecture, and religion as well as packet boats, plantations, and other aspects of economic life.

MUSIC IN AMERICA.   MENC Handbook

This features such outstanding musical personalities as Marian Anderson, George Gershwin, Benny Goodman, Mischa Elman, and Serge Koussevitsky. It shows how jazz was derived from Negro folk music and how Gershwin was inspired by this popular idiom of his time.

THAT MAN SAMSON.   Bell and Howell Company.

Creative Activities

Make up dances for Negro music and for jazz rhythms. Write original dsecants for such songs as "Swing Low, Sweet Chariot."

Have several string basses brought to class. Encourage several of the group to "thump" the bass for accompaniment. Open strings can be used on songs like "Shortnin' Bread", "There's a Little Wheel A-Turnin' " etc.

A minstrel show could be a natural outgrowth of this unit and dances could be created, costumes designed, an original script with an interlocutor written, etc.

Other Activities

Study the lives of famous Negro personalities such as James Bland, Marian Anderson, Dorothy Maynor, Katherine Dunham, Nathaniel Dett, and Roland Hayes.

Study the lives of other great Negroes such as George Washington Carver, Booker T. Washington, James Weldon Johnson, Jesse Owens, and Dr. Charles Drew.

Study the styles of jazz band leaders.

Insert appropriate pictures and favorite rhythm patterns in notebooks. Include a tracing of the history of the development of jazz.

Music Reading Assignments

Lomax, John A. and Alan. AMERICAN BALLADS AND FOLK SONGS. The Macmillan Company, New York, 1934.

> *Creole, Mountain, White Minstrel, etc.*   Pages 211-299
> *Spirituals*   Pages 577-610

Van Loon, Hendrik Willem. THE ARTS. Simon and Schuster, New York, 1937.

> *Chopin, The Originator of the Modern*
> *Nationalistic "Blues"*   Page 609

Hartshorn, Leavitt. AT HOME AND ABROAD. (Making Friends with Music). Ginn and Company, Chicago, 1940.

> *Bess, You Is My Woman Now*   Page 42
> *Rhapsody in Blue*   Page 39

Carter, Phyllis Anne. THE BANDS PLAY ON. Robert M. Mcbride and Company, New York, 1942.

> *Today's Bands and Orchestras*   Chapter XI